VIDEO MODELING
A VISUAL TEACHING METHOD FOR CHILDREN WITH AUTISM

Revised and Updated Second Edition

LIISA NEUMANN

WILLERIK PUBLISHING
Brandon, Florida

Published in the United States by:
WILLERIK PUBLISHING
P.O. Box 6692, Brandon, Florida 33508

This book is sold with the understanding that the author is not engaged in professional service. It is designed to provide information in regard to the use of video modeling to educate children with autism. The reader is urged to exercise caution in using the described techniques. The services of a professional person should be sought for expert opinion or legal advice.

ISBN: 0-615-11310-9

Printed in the United States of America

This is dedicated to...

my son, William, for whom I will continue to turn the world upside down in search of a cure for autism.

ACKNOWLEDGMENTS

A very special acknowledgment goes to my son Erik who has been my very best *actor* for my video modeling lessons. He is also now a skilled cameraman and understands the tenets of good video modeling. Throughout my learning curve, he has been incredibly patient with having a mother and a *director.*

I am especially grateful to Mary Barbera, a colleague and friend, who has been instrumental in getting this 2nd edition more thoroughly organized and expanded. She is highly regarded in the field of education and has tremendous respect for children with autism. I am very fortunate to have been able to benefit from her wealth of knowledge and wisdom.

During the two years that I worked at Anne Arundel County Public Schools in Maryland teaching autistic preschoolers, I had the good fortune to work with two very dedicated people, Barbara Flook and Jean Dunaway. Working as a team, we were able to use video modeling successfully with our students and share the technique with families and other educators. Having had the opportunity to see video modeling work so well with other autistic children gave me the confidence to present this technique nationally and to get to work on the second edition.

This second edition and William's leaps in learning wouldn't be possible were it not for the Hillsborough County Public School team in Florida that is working with him now, especially Shannon Les Perance, Sylvia Corrica, Kathryn Rhoades, Suzanne Motl, Steve Sims, Aurora Colaianni, Marci Brewster, Donna Myers, and Francisca Olson.

William's 4th grade regular education teacher, Kathryn Rhoades, his speech and language pathologist, Sylvia Corrica, his exceptional student education coordinator, Shannon Les Perance, and his special education teacher, Suzanne Motl give new meaning to the concept of excellence in education. They are successfully managing his aversion to learning so that he is learning and are challenging him like he's never been challenged before.

Thank you also to William's many good friends in regular education in Maryland who were really some of his best educators, especially Samantha Gage, who was even inspired to write a book (Runaway William). All of his regular education classmates in Florida have made William feel welcome, but from the first day, his classmate Terry has been his strongest supporter and best friend.

I would also like to give thanks to my husband for his compassion and support in facing the joys and heartaches of autism with me, to my mother and father for their faithful support and help in editing and publishing this guide, to my good friend, Mary Noy, who helped to edit the second edition, to Jan Jones and Mary Hepple for having been part of the original IEP team, and to the many friends and family members who have said "what a great idea!"

And a special thank you to the people at Anne Arundel County Public Schools in Maryland that first helped to make video modeling a reality at school for my son and subsequently for other children with autism. They continue to inspire me to write, present and develop the technique of video modeling, especially Pat Anderson, Barbara Flook, Pam Courson, Martha Walker, Gladys Burgess, Carol Schwalm, Bonnie Russell, and Tom Conner. Through William's toughest times they persevered for him. They recognized William's capabilities and my determination to help him.

I would also like to offer my sincere appreciation to regular and special education teachers, support staff and administrators, *everywhere*, who are willing to *act,* first by being actors and actresses in videos and second by acting on and supporting the concept of video modeling.

TABLE OF CONTENTS

Using the Camcorder
Acting
Writing the Scripts
Videotaping the Lesson
Building in Practice Time
Videotaping the Reward or Reinforcer
Viewing the Video with Your Child

Preparing for Medical Procedures
Presentations
Pretend Play
Reading
Requesting
Riding a Bike and Braking
Riding Public Transportation
Rote Conversation
Rote Questions & Answers
Safety
Science & Social Studies
Shapes
Sitting at a Desk
Spelling
Surroundings
Toileting
Turn Taking
Writing
Yes/No Questions

FOREWORD

Video Modeling Made Fun, Easy, and Effective!

While searching the Cure Autism Now website a few years ago, I learned about the original edition of Liisa Neumann's book on video modeling. At the website I found a report about an "Innovative Technology Conference" held in 2000. The report included an account of Liisa's demonstration of the video modeling programs created for her son with autism. The demonstration was quite a hit and the report described it as "one of the simplest and most practical innovative technologies on display." Readers were also encouraged to check out Liisa's book at her website. I did and promptly ordered several copies. I then shared the book with students and colleagues who were actively involved in delivering services to children with autism spectrum disorders. Just reading about the video modeling programs led us to agree with the conference report's positive review. This new edition of the book improves upon a really good thing; I am delighted to have the opportunity to endorse it.

This book is an inspiring account of how Liisa has used video modeling over the years to help her son learn communication, play, social, academic, and self-help skills, as well as "to overcome numerous fears and phobias." As Liisa put it, "Having read about and tried all sorts of therapies... we found one that was and continues to be fun (for William and us), easy, and effective." Liisa ran into something that worked with her son – she discovered that video modeling caused a little learning to take place and immediately went to work exploring its potential for causing a lot of learning to take place. We are fortunate that she takes the time to share her discoveries with us.

Liisa's illustrations and recommendations corroborate the views of others who suggest that video modeling can be a valuable supplement to other forms of teaching: (a) video modeling can expose a learner to multiple examples of instructional cues difficult to orchestrate otherwise; (b) such cues can increase attention to relevant cues; (c) a teacher can tailor the instructional cues for maximum impact on the learner; (d) a teacher has flexibility in when, where, and how often learning opportunities occur; (e) motivation for learning may be enhanced because imitating what others do and say appears intrinsically rewarding for some students; and (f) video modeling may increase the cost efficiency of a child's individualized programming.

Discovering Liisa's work is important for my colleagues and me because of a commitment to translate our research into practical teaching tools that try to leverage the benefits of video modeling. To succeed, we recognize the need to appreciate the practical context for our work as thoroughly as possible. Liisa's work provides us with important insights into the art and practice of teaching with video modeling in everyday circumstances. If approached with the skill, wisdom, and creative energy expressed in her book, the use of video modeling by parents, practitioners, and researchers could indeed be fun, easy, and effective. I urge others to give the techniques described in this gem a try. In the end, the learning of many children with autism spectrum disorders and other special needs could be vastly improved.

Robert Stromer, Ph.D.
University of Massachusetts Medical School
Shriver Center

William (right) from fearful to relaxed and enjoying steam engines.

A PERSONAL MESSAGE

I have the good fortune of writing this revised and updated second edition from the Tampa Bay area in Florida. For various reasons, including our son William's education, we decided to relocate to Florida, a state that has dual enrollment. This means that William can attend school for part of the day and be home schooled for the rest.

For too many years in Maryland, William's learned behaviors varied on a seasonal basis. For example, he learned to overcome his fear of flying insects and scurrying animals only to have the stimulus die off or fly south for the winter. Being fearful of being outside is very limiting to the course of human development. Moreover, in order for William to further develop his language and social skills, we felt he needed to get more practice talking and engaging people than he needed to learn to sit and work quietly. It was just a matter of balancing his needs differently.

Dual enrollment allows our son, William, to take advantage of the best the public school system has to offer along with having the opportunity to spend more time learning at home and in the community. In Florida, the best the public system has to offer started with a half day consisting of differentiated instruction provided by the regular education teacher in an inclusive setting, interaction with typically developing peers in a school where respect, responsibility and character building are of the utmost importance, daily speech and language therapy provided by an exceptional speech therapist, and a reading recovery program that is making a difference. As we get to know the school, we are finding that it has the treasure trove of opportunities we have always been looking for.

William has adjusted to his new school and, for the time being, is responding to his regular education teachers and classmates without added adult support. They are taking a lead role in including him. His special education teacher, language and occupational therapists are working tirelessly behind the scenes to close the gaps. Everyone is building on his abilities. The focus is not on his disability. And therefore, both William and I have confidence in their abilities. He is genuinely happy in school.

Due to the tropical climate in Florida, William has also quickly learned to live with fire ants, dragonflies, lizards, bees, and birds, including the ones migrating from up north. They are a year round reality in Florida. He has a greater part of his day available for practicing talking and communicating. And, video modeling is back in his routine. From this sunnier place, we continue to evaluate and educate William on an ongoing basis as his symptoms vary from month to month and year to year. Autism is not a static condition.

Change can be a challenge for children with autism. Relocating to Florida was a scary prospect due to all the impending changes, but it has been well worth the risk. William has opportunities to learn and grow that are unrivaled in his past.

I hope this personal message adds to your understanding of our approach to managing autism and the concept of reaching and teaching beyond the boundaries. *And remember, though it may be difficult at times, teaching children with autism is a privilege.* There is no greater reward than the progress of a developing child.

Liisa Neumann

A RATIONALE FOR VIDEO MODELING

Diagnosing autism in children at a young age is a complicated process and the treatment is even more complex from both the medical and educational standpoints. To add to that, financial constraints for many families and school systems can be limiting factors to considering treatment alternatives. Unfortunately, the prevalence of autism seems to be increasing. It is now estimated to occur in approximately 1 in 294 individuals (Center for Disease Control Autism Prevalence Study for Metropolitan Atlanta, 2002). Whether this is an increase in the incidence or an increase in the identification of autism still needs to be sorted out.

Although autism is a disability with diagnostic criteria, it is also a spectrum disorder. This means that no two children with autism will have identical autistic characteristics: some are verbal, some are non-verbal, some have social skills, some have no social skills; some have repetitive behaviors, some do not. What many of these children do have in common is that they are visual, rather than auditory learners. Regardless of these differences, autistic children also have unique strengths and abilities. For over six years, our son's regular education *classmates* have embraced William as a friend, regularly complimenting and encouraging him. These children who see and focus on the *friend* in having a friend with autism will one day be our decision makers. That is a lesson in itself.

If you really think about it, most people have at least some traits that may be regarded as autistic. By autistic trait, it is simply meant that a person has a difference in an area of communication, socialization, stereotypic behavior or restricted interests. Have you ever seen someone make a Freudian slip or have difficulty with word recall (communication), play a great song over and over, or twirl their hair, or tap their feet (stereotypic behavior), or daydream or be shy (socialization), or get obsessed with work, have an intense interest and ability in memorizing video game facts (restricted interest) or perseverate, in other words persisting in a purpose, idea, or task in the face of perceived obstacles?

For most of us these habits or traits are insignificant and do not necessarily interfere with daily living, but they would take a fair amount of effort or intervention to stop or change. Such characteristics just make us all different. Children with autism, however, tend to have more variability in these characteristics, which can interfere with daily living. In order to find the most appropriate method of changing some of these autistic traits and thereby helping to further along their education, parents and educators have a formidable challenge.

Having read about and tried all sorts of therapies, it was not until the summer of 1997, that we found one that was and continues to be fun (for William and us), easy, and effective. We were videotaping our two boys, Erik and William, playing in the backyard pool. Erik was 6 ½ years old and William, our child with autism, was almost 5 years old. Erik was doggy paddling and trying desperately to get himself on top of a huge pool ball. William, not knowing how to swim, was laughing at Erik's attempts to get on the ball. Later the same day, we sat down to watch the video. William thought the video was hysterically funny. He wanted to see it over and over, as he does with videos he likes. The next day, William couldn't wait to get in the pool. Within minutes, William was on the pool ball, purposefully falling off and splashing and otherwise laughing and being very proud of himself. We were very surprised, but not as surprised as when he spontaneously started doggy paddling. William had taught himself how to swim simply by watching a home video. Right then, I knew we had a means (video modeling) to teach him much, much more.

For three months prior to this experience, we had been exhausting ourselves with a moderately intensive behavioral intervention program, discrete trial training, using the principles of applied behavior analysis (ABA). This type of program can be very costly as it typically requires thirty or more hours of one-to-one instruction for the child and a significant amount of professional review and training for the one-to-one therapists.

Mostly for financial reasons and time constraints, we opted for a modified program. Without a money-back guarantee, it seemed like too much to invest in one methodology. Some professionals cite the term recovery in describing their methods and programs. This can be a lure. For most children it's really not recovery that is needed. Recovery implies a loss. It is more accurately a developmental level of progress that is needed. Where the bar and expectations are set determines the level. So, in setting out to close the gap between William's chronological age and his developmental level, we maintained William in an early childhood intervention preschool classroom and I was the one-to-one assistant at home, providing as many hours as I could fit into my otherwise hectic schedule. William definitely began learning at a quicker pace. Nevertheless, we had to repeat each question and prompt each answer hundreds of times, and with lots of enthusiasm, to get him to remember each new word. That was tiring.

After seeing William's response to the swimming video, I was confident that if I videotaped a particular question and answer and played it for him over and over, he would be able to memorize the question and answer more quickly than in the traditional one-to-one instructional method. He, like many children with autism, has an exceptional memory, especially for videos. I knew, however, that William would not focus on any video unless it had something that interested him, in his case trains.

The success of video modeling is largely dependent on featuring a reinforcer (the reward) that is of great interest to the child (such as trains, cars, planes, dolls, animals, spinning toys) after the lesson. I simply videotaped the lesson and then added a few minutes of train play at the end. It worked like magic. After William had watched the short video between 5-10 times, he had memorized the names of the objects. At that point, I gradually switched over to using video modeling for introducing lessons and used the one-to-one time to practice the skills modeled on video. So, his educational programming was no longer limited to discrete trial training and preschool. It also included video modeling and interaction with his then six-year-old brother, the actor in the videos with whom he would practice the lessons and play with. We also applied the principles of behavior management (an attempt at perfect parenting) throughout the day.

During the past six years, we have definitely improved our skill at video modeling. We have also learned that there are few limits to what you can teach with video modeling. Through trial and error, we have figured out what works. Before we started using video modeling, William didn't really seem to understand my voice. He didn't know the alphabet, numbers, colors, or shapes. His expressive vocabulary was limited to less than twenty-five words. He couldn't repeat a two-word combination, such as eight-five, let alone a string of numbers such as his telephone number. And, he refused to write.

By using video modeling as an adjunct tool to good teaching, William has learned to understand most of what people say to him. From time to time, he does still use the behavior management principle of "planned ignoring." He was born a master of behavior management. As a toddler, he successfully worked screaming to his advantage, until we started fighting back with our own behavioral management strategies, which did not include screaming back. We have discovered that he is a young man with determination, which if channeled to good use will serve him well.
Now, he is doing simple math. He is reading and writing without tantrumming. He uses attributes to describe what he wants. He comments. His articulation is greatly improved, his expressive vocabulary is significant and he has the ability to talk in short sentences and even negotiate a little. Video modeling has also helped William to overcome numerous fears and phobias. While he is not at grade level, he has made significant progress, particularly during the years when video modeling was used more aggressively.

The public school system was also impressed with William's progress using video modeling. In his earlier years, we were able to show his teachers and key people at the Board of Education in Maryland that William could learn using this method where he had been struggling before. During kindergarten through third grade, his teachers built video modeling into his daily routine.

When William was in kindergarten, I started by asking the special educator to give me a handful of activities that William was struggling with (I think that was just about everything) to see if I could teach him the material with video models. I made a video model for him and let him watch it for a few days. By the end of the week, he had mastered most of the skills. I could have just as easily used unmet individualized education plan (IEP) goals. I shared the video with William's special educator. I believe she was impressed as she brought it to the attention of the IEP team and from then on it was a part of William's schedule.

William's teacher further developed the use of video modeling by introducing structured practice time between the lesson and the reward. After the lesson, the video displayed the word "work" on a 3 x 5 card for five minutes. During this time his teacher or teaching assistant practiced the lesson with him. The cycle repeated with another five minute lesson, five minutes of practice time, and a five minute reward.

At school, video modeling gave William a break from the demands of group and one-to-one activities. He understood that he needed to finish his classroom work so that he could watch a video and that he needed to watch the first part of the video (the lesson) to watch the second part of the video (the reward). William's day still alternates between preferred and non-preferred activities. Although most educational activities remain non-preferred, video modeling time is an educational activity that is preferred.

For a period of two years in Maryland, the type of video modeling William was exposed to varied. Unfortunately, he was featured in some of the school videos, the practice time became less structured, and the reward element of the video was eliminated, all well intended. At home, some of my videos lacked the pizzazz of my earlier videos. So, I asked the school to discontinue the use of video modeling and went back to making the kinds of videos William really loves to watch – those featuring train crashes and disasters for rewards.

Watching videos is enjoyable for William, so it makes learning fun. William doesn't have to be continually redirected to the lesson because videos hold his attention. If he's not paying attention to the video, I revise the lesson and retape. If he hasn't learned the lesson after watching a video 5-10 times, it's not his fault that he's not learning, it's my fault that I'm not teaching properly. Teaching is defined as imparting knowledge or causing learning to occur. If the knowledge does not impart in a reasonable amount of time, the teaching needs review. Sometimes I need to modify the lesson to make it more discrete or meaningful. Other times I need to include a more interesting or motivating reward.

Although William is learning more readily now, we continue to use video modeling at home for subject areas and issues that are more difficult for him. It is an enjoyable way to unwind while also developing his understanding of our world.

So while researchers, pediatricians and educators continue to practice in their respective fields, for William's sake, I am continuing my development of video modeling. It is efficient, effective, affordable, and fun for both of us.

INTRODUCTION TO THE USE OF VIDEO MODELING

Video modeling for children with autism is a method of educating children by modeling lessons on video with the intention of affecting changes in behavior. For the purposes of this discussion, the term behavior refers to all actions and reactions. This includes the gamut of all verbal and non-verbal actions and reactions. Our internal dialogue is also a behavior. Furthermore, the absence of an action or reaction is also a behavior. By modeling behaviors on videotape in a purposeful and often discrete manner, the child learns to memorize, imitate, and generalize (appropriately adapt) the behaviors.

Video modeling, used as a means to modify, change, or shape behavior, is appropriate for use at home and school. It is also a convenient method for developing or strengthening the home-school connection, simply by sending the videos back and forth. It may increase the effectiveness of existing treatment programs. And, it may offer a way of *getting through* to your child with autism when getting through seems impossible.

Video modeling can result in two simple forms of videos– good and bad. Good videos are the result of constant analysis of the specific behaviors that are being targeted and the application of a plan to effect the change. For some parents and educators this comes naturally and it's easy. For others, a refresher on human behavior and development in general, not necessarily specific to autism, is helpful. Without a good understanding of human behavior and development, it is possible to make bad videos and thereby worsen some of the autistic characteristics.

Most of the symptoms of autism are essentially manifestations of behavior (see figure 1). If we can affect the behavior of a child with autism, with video modeling or any other methodology, we are essentially treating symptoms of autism. Although the symptoms may be caused by biologic conditions, they basically manifest as variations in behavior. It is not surprising that applied behavioral analysis (ABA) is thought to be one of the most effective treatments by many autism professionals. In fact, it is now considered a mainstream treatment. Essentially, we all use degrees of ABA with our typical children because it works. It is acceptable to use intervention when a child exhibits good or bad behavior, such as offering a special dinner out for a good report card or using time-out for foul language. If the intervention is effective, the bad behavior ceases or decreases and the desirable behavior increases.

SOME COMMON BEHAVIORS
ASSOCIATED WITH AUTISM…

Little or no eye contact
Difficulty with transitions and change
Tantrums
Language delays
Unresponsive
Acts as if deaf
Lack of gesturing or pointing to express needs
Echolalia (repeating words or phrases)
Laughing or crying for reasons not apparent to
others
Difficulty in socialization
Unusual, repetitive play
Lines up or spins objects
Unaffectionate or overly affectionate
Unresponsive to traditional teaching methods
Inappropriate attachment to objects
Gazing at objects in an unusual manner
Unusual sensitivity to pain
Inability to understand danger
Hyperactivity or under activity
Splinter (uneven) skill development

*This list of behaviors is informational and not intended
to be used for diagnostic purposes*

Figure 1

By instinctively analyzing changes in behavior, we learn how to manage the behavior of our children. We recognize that a consequence (or proactively an antecedent) was effective and continue to use it until it doesn't work anymore, then we find another consequence (or antecedent). This type of intervention is standard form. It is not viewed as intervention, but is called good parenting or good schooling. It is generally thought to be more effective to be proactive in developing good behavior than to be reactive to bad behavior.

Children with autism also need this type of ABA intervention - *analyze the behavior and apply a plan* (this is a clearer way to describe applied behavior analysis). The difference is that the behaviors can vary further from norms. This can make analyzing the behaviors and developing and applying intervention plans more difficult.

As a result of the ongoing development of new therapies to help autistic children, autism has been somewhat commercialized. Many excellent practices have been developed; however, there is wide disagreement on the effectiveness of available educational methodologies. Parents and educators, therefore, face difficult decisions in choosing between costly therapies.

Applied behavior analysis, in broad terms, is a way of life. There are many people that use the term applied behavioral analysis synonymously with discrete trial training. This is an unfortunate confusion in terminology. ABA is the common thread that runs through all methods of educating our children. Discrete trial training, a common technique used as a part of so-called ABA programs, can be very effective for some children, but is also very costly. It is thought to be dependent on beginning intervention at a very early age and to require 30-40 hours per week of one-to-one instruction by a therapist other than the parent. This inherently excludes the majority of children with autism because, at this point, many pediatricians are not diagnosing autism early enough and the cost of 30-40 hours of intervention per week is prohibitive for most families.

There is no question that progress requires interaction and intervention for all children. The difficulty for parents and educators of children with autism is deciding how to diversify the portfolio of methodologies for the waking hours of a toddler or child. Fortunately, there is a movement toward earlier diagnosis and growing public school support of behavioral intervention or ABA for children with autism.

Used as an adjunct tool to almost any program, video modeling is a way for parents and educators to begin or help in intervening. It is a simple way of communicating to a child that what they are seeing on the television or computer is what you want them to do. The lessons being taught both at home and in most treatment programs can be modeled on videotape.

Although every child is unique, there are three differentiating traits among children with autism that are very common that make them candidates for video modeling. First, they tend to be *visual* learners as opposed to auditory learners. Second, like many of us, they excel when routines are *predictable* and repetitious. And third, again like many of us, they are assertive and like *control.* By working with and not against these traits, parents and educators can encourage the development of social, academic, and communication skills (good behaviors). The key to changing old behaviors and developing new behaviors is to consistently and systematically intervene, basing the interventions on the unique qualities of the child.

---

1. Make it Visual

2. Make it Predictable

3. Share some Control

A typical child can process auditory instructions without much difficulty. Often, a child with autism can process the same information if the verbal instruction is paired with visual cues. For example, by repeatedly providing a picture schedule along with an explanation of the activities planned for a school day, a child with autism may be able to follow the routine with his peers more readily. The picture symbols provide a concrete way to give meaning to a word or expression (the picture is confined within a space as in a photograph). It has boundaries. The difficulty may arise in maintaining the attention of the child, while simultaneously pairing the visual and auditory stimuli (the picture symbol with the verbal cues).

There is a medium in which the visual and auditory stimuli are automatically paired and the information is presented in a concrete format – the television and computer. However, most television and computer programs designed for the average child are overwhelming for children with autism. The language level and speed are generally too advanced and the picture is typically cluttered with visual and auditory distractions. Although many children with autism do not learn well from these television and computer programs, certain television and computer programs can hold our children's *attention* much better and longer than we can, even given the language speed and visual distractions.

Hollywood's ability to capture our interest and the commercial use of videos for such diverse applications as repairing homes, cooking, exercising, model railroading, and learning foreign *languages* gives further merit to the effectiveness of the video medium. We have something to learn from the Hollywood film industry's ability to hold our children's interest – learning to write screenplays and being great cameramen, actors, directors and producers.

The camcorder gives parents and educators a means to do this. We can individualize the pairing of the *visual* with the auditory stimuli, while controlling the distractions of the real world. Watching a video repeatedly is *predictable*. And, by pairing a lesson with a reward, the child has some *control* in knowing that he will get what he wants (the reward). Furthermore, we can act, direct, produce and playback instantly.

> A **visual** intervention that also provides **predictability** and **control**, such as video modeling, is likely to be a successful means to intervene.

Predictability is more difficult to achieve in a one-to-one setting than in a video model. A therapist, educator, teaching assistant or parent cannot possibly control all the variables in the teaching environment so that the lesson is repeated in exactly the same manner all of the time. For example, if a therapist is trying to teach the color red, a child with autism may be overly distracted by a single change in the surroundings (such as a sticky spill on the table, a cracker crumb, a change in the weather, a different assortment of educational materials next to the therapist). The color red, as learned the day before, may now be a totally different color in the mind of the child with autism because the color is paired with a change in the surroundings. Given these circumstances, it may take an unusually long time to learn the color red.

On the other hand, when a video is playing on the television screen, the lesson, learning the color red, is being taught in a concrete form (within the boundaries of the television screen). The lesson is identical each time. It is predictable. If the video was recorded with a small crumb next to the color red, then the color red is easier to learn because nothing is changing around it during the initial memorization phase. After the child has seen the video a number of times and has memorized the answer, it is more likely that the child will adapt his understanding of the color red, irrespective of changes in the surroundings.

There are many advantages to video modeling. By virtue of its predictability, video modeling can help to desensitize children with autism to stressful conditions. This may be one of the reasons why it helps to make other interventions more effective. By placing the teacher or parent within the confines of a television, a child can also focus on the lesson without the distraction of human interaction (including voice modulation, body movements, good or bad breath, perfume and cologne changes, different clothing and accessories, and hairstyle changes). Nevertheless, video modeling is not a substitute for one-to-one interaction, nor is it a cure. *Video modeling is simply a way to introduce lessons.*

As many children with autism can remember and echo movie scripts with relative ease, video modeling can be used to change behavior by teaching in a memorable way. Memory is different in everyone. If we want our children to learn, it is important to make the lessons memorable. Video modeling, being an impressionable teaching method, can also be used to tailor echolalia to a more functional purpose. This is accomplished by personalizing the scripted language in the videos.

Another advantage of video modeling is that your child has access to the materials presented on the video. Unlike in the commercial educational videos, the materials are right at home or in the classroom. Therefore, if your child wants to practice manipulating the materials and the corresponding language, they are readily accessible to him. If your child decides to practice the lessons on his own, this frees up more time for you. As there is little added cost involved, if a camcorder, television and video cassette recorder are already available, video modeling can save money for families and schools. And as almost all children love to watch videos, especially of themselves, their friends and their belongings, parents and educators may find children seeking opportunities to learn.

The video models are not time consuming to make. The first few will likely take longer as you get comfortable with this technique. On average, a 15-20 minute video model takes approximately 40-45 minutes to videotape. This includes the time needed to gather materials and rehearse the script. The process of making videos can be easy or complicated. This depends on the approach. The basic functions of most camcorders are quite simple. The level of editing that is employed will affect the complexity of the process. The basic video model can go right from camcorder to television without editing.

With video modeling, you are also able to be an objective observer while your child is learning. You are no longer part of the subjective teacher-student interaction. The teacher has the opportunity to observe for student interest while the videotape plays. Without interest in the lesson, a child is less likely to learn. Encouraging and motivating a child to be interested in a video can help. Forcing a child to watch a video is not recommended as this can cause the teaching method, video modeling, to become unpleasant and aversive for the child.

And last, but not least, video modeling can help resolve some of the helplessness and hopelessness felt by extended family members, friends, and educators. Everyone can have a successful part in video modeling, from being an actor to camera person to prop assistant.

An environment in which learning is enjoyable is almost certain to be successful. In this guide, you will learn how easy it is for anyone (parents, educators, relatives and friends) to effectively educate children with autism by using video modeling. And if successful, this guide may also spark your creative genius in helping to further develop the art of video modeling.

While the scope of this edition is at the preschool and elementary school levels, application of these techniques with older children, adults, and at higher levels of intellectual development may also be effective. The efficacy of video modeling in the higher levels of intellectual development will likely be dependent on the child reaching a point where learning is more incidental to less discrete teaching and the desire to learn is more fully developed.

IMPORTANT NOTICE

As video modeling can be a powerful method of developing imitative behavior, be cautious not to video objects or activities that would be dangerous for your child to do, touch or use without adult supervision. If the video model is effective, your child may want to practice the lesson, even without an adult present. It is important to limit video modeling to activities that do not pose a danger to the child. Dangerous situations include, but are not limited to, touching or turning on the stove, turning on a hair dryer near water (electric shock hazard), swimming in a pool, using utensils (particularly a knife), bathing, using the microwave oven, and using power tools. Furthermore, as your child learns to imitate from videos, it will be important to monitor and control the television programs your child watches for the very same reason that we are all encouraged to monitor and control our children's exposure to television, the possibility that the child may decide to imitate inappropriately. Teaching judgment is a life-long process.

WHAT TO VIDEO

It's up to you. There are many good resources from which to develop a video modeling lesson plan. They may include the goals and objectives from an existing assessment or individualized education plan, your observations on areas that need improvement, and curriculum guides offered in books and periodicals on autism. A good teacher, behavior consultant, speech therapist or friend may also be able to help with developing appropriate objectives. The behaviors that you choose to address may be in the area of communication, self-help, socialization, attention, stereotypic behavior, emotional development, restricted interests, academics, and so on.

By either informally or formally analyzing the child's behavior and prioritizing these behaviors, the lesson will begin to take shape. For example, if in observing the child you notice that he runs to the door when the doorbell rings, but runs off without greeting the guest, the lesson may involve three steps: walking towards the door, opening the door and shaking hands, and then closing the door.

It is important to develop a long-range plan. Typically, this is for a period of six months to one year. However, it is equally important to pay attention to your daily observations as these may affect the course of your plan. In attempting to teach particular skills, you may encounter *stumbling blocks* to learning. These *stumbling blocks* then become the answer to "what to video." This is a natural way to analyze and consequently break down lessons into more discrete pieces, as needed. For example, the objective may be to slide down a slide. If the child develops a fear of going outside, addressing and overcoming that fear may be the first step to getting to the slide to work on that objective.

The steps involved in making videos and the process of using video modeling will also affect the lesson plan. For example, if you have decided that teaching the social behaviors involved in going to a restaurant are a priority, but you do not have the means to practice going to a restaurant, your time may be better spent on another lesson. Similarly, if you decide to teach the names of objects in the house or at school, you will want to focus the lesson on objects that are accessible in a quiet room (away from a running dishwasher, hairdryer, or pager system).

The advantage of addressing objectives on the individualized education plan or objectives developed from an assessment is that the child may demonstrate a higher capacity for learning to the teacher or therapist. Once the goals and objectives of a plan are met, it's time for a new plan.

A good data collection system is a key and essential element to figuring out which teaching methods are suited to your child. Without a data collection system, it is possible that the successes and failures of video modeling could inadvertently mask both ineffective and effective teaching strategies being used by both parents and educators. For example, if the data shows that a child is learning sight words quickly from video models, then working one-on-one, trial after trial, may not be time well spent for teaching this skill. Similarly, if one-to-one instruction is being used successfully to engage a child in a dialogue, then rote video models of conversation may not be a good use of time. If video modeling, one-to-one and group instruction are all being used to teach, then a record of which teaching method, independent of the other, results in quicker skill acquisition and generalization is important to maintain. One method may affect quicker acquisition and another may result in more effective generalization.

Without gathering data, it is difficult to plan for the efficient use of time for both you and the child. In working with special needs children, time is of the essence as the number of school years available to the child is limited. It is important to collect and analyze data, so that you carefully choose what to video. Then, progress can be maximized.

There are many ways to gather data, which can be helpful to efficient lesson planning. The criterion for each video needs to be set incrementally and in a manner which ensures the child can learn successfully. For example, meeting the prerequisite criterion of knowing how to open a book and turn pages is one essential step toward being successful at meeting the criterion of reading at the 1st grade level.

In collecting data, first and foremost, we need to measure the child's progress. Very simply, during practice time keep a record (perhaps next to the written script) of the level of mastery of the skill at the criteria level that was set. Generally speaking, eighty to one hundred percent (an A or a B) is considered mastery. Second and simultaneously, measure your progress in teaching the skill. This is accomplished by keeping a record of the number of times you presented the lesson before the skill was acquired. If the child has watched the video five times and is showing improvement, you may decide to show the video another five times. On the other hand, if after watching the video five times, your child won't engage in the practice activity, you can give yourself a zero and change the delivery of the lesson.

Ultimately, data drives the lesson. If your data shows that a lesson was ineffective, then it's time to modify the delivery of the lesson. And likewise, if your data shows that the child has mastered the lesson, it is time to raise the bar with a new lesson.

Cartoon designed by Erik, William's best friend and older brother, to demonstrate the concept that progress in education is dependent on data analysis.

IDEAS FOR WHAT TO VIDEO

Actions
Alphabet
Appropriate Play
Art Projects
Articulation or Pronunciation
Attention to People, Work and Games
Bathing
Coins & Currency
Colors
Cultural Arts Activities (Art, Music, PE)
Cutting with Scissors, Gluing, Coloring
Dressing
Eating a Meal
Emotions
Environmental Sounds
Fears
Functions of Objects
Going Places
Greetings
Grooming
Hands Down or Hands Quiet
I Don't Know as an Answer
I see vs. I have
Identifying Rooms
Manners (Excuse Me, Please & Thank You)
Matching
Math

Music
Name
Naming Objects
Numbers
Opposites
Parts of the Body
Pencil Grip
People
Physical Education Activities
Preparing for Medical Procedures
Prepositions
Presentations
Pretend Play
Pronouns
Reading
Requesting
Riding a Bike & Braking
Riding Public Transportation
Rote Conversations
Rote Questions & Answers
Science & Social Studies
Shapes
Sitting at a Desk
Social Situations
Spelling
Surroundings & Community
Toileting
Turn-Taking
Tying Shoes
Waiting
Writing and Pressing Lightly/Firmly
Yes/No Questions

HOW TO MAKE
A SUCCESSFUL VIDEO

The basics of videotaping for the purpose of educating are simple. The key principle is to make learning enjoyable by alternating the lesson (the non-preferred activity) with the reward or reinforcer (the preferred activity). In order to see the preferred activity, your child will have to tune into the non-preferred activity. Until there is a well-developed desire to learn, the lesson will need a reward. This is not unusual. We all work for pay. You will know when the desire develops because the lesson will be as interesting as the reward is to the child. This desire may be variable depending on the subject matter.

There are seven important aspects to creating a successful video. They are the following: using the camcorder and being the cameraman, acting, directing and producing, writing the scripts, the lesson, practice time, the reward or reinforcer, and viewing the video with your child. As editing can complicate the video making process for the parent or educator, the focus of this discussion is on getting from camcorder to television, and therefore from teaching to learning, as effortlessly as possible.

USING THE CAMCORDER and BEING THE CAMERA PERSON: The following are some basic tips that may be helpful when filming.

- Hold the camcorder steady and move slowly. For some viewers, erratic and sudden movements can cause motion sickness.

- Avoid using a tripod. A little bit of movement will give the video a more real appearance.

- Eliminate distractions by turning off noisy appliances and ensuring that everyone knows to be quiet while the video is being recorded. Air handlers in schools can be very noisy. Limit visual distractions by zooming in on the subject or object.

- To videotape yourself, enlist the help of another person if possible. If not, use a tripod or set the camera on a table. Use a remote control device, if you have one.

- To direct attention, hold the camcorder with one hand and point with the other hand to the subject (or use a pointer). Zoom in, as necessary.

- If your child is right handed, hold the camcorder with your left hand and manipulate materials with your right hand. If you child is left handed, videotape with your right hand and manipulate materials with your left hand.

- To give perspective, where possible, manipulate materials with one hand and videotape with the other. This way, your child will see the actual perspective of the activity. He will have the precise image in his mind of the distance from his eyes and hands to the object. For example, I have been able to rest a child's book on my lap, videotape and read simultaneously, while pointing to the words. Other examples include writing lessons or playing appropriately with toys.

- You may find that it is helpful to practice manipulating materials, rehearsing the script and operating the camcorder before you push *record*.

- Videotape at your child's eye level. If your child is two feet tall, then get down to the two-foot level. If your child is five feet tall, videotape at the five-foot level.

- The advantage to using a digital video camera is that you can print photos from your videos and use them as visual cues to the material learned on the video. For example, if you videotaped a *going to a restaurant video*, you could isolate and print a short sequence of events to follow, in the form of a schedule, during the restaurant visit.

- For hands on activities which you can't videotape with one hand and manipulate the material with the other, videotape over the shoulder of your actor in order to model the activity from the child's perspective.

- As the *camera person*, for the purpose of teaching with video modeling, do not videotape anyone (including the child with autism) engaged in the behaviors you are trying to eliminate or change.

ACTING, DIRECTING AND PRODUCING: Just like in Hollywood, there are important aspects to creating a movie or video.

- When selecting your actor(s), keep a close watch on who your child likes to see on video. Although William doesn't mind hearing my voice on the videos, he doesn't usually like to see me on the videos. On the other hand, William thoroughly enjoys watching his father and brother. They could just sit on the front porch and make funny faces. It wouldn't take long for William to figure out how to imitate their funny face making antics even without a reinforcer.

- Peer models of the same age make good actors. Erik, William's brother, has been our best actor. To encourage Erik to act his best, we put him on an incentive program…we reward him less for the short scenes and a little more for the longer, more complex scripts.

- Retake a scene if you feel you have made a mistake in the way the video is presented or if your child might interpret the lesson too literally. It is much easier to rewind and rerecord right away than to try to "unteach" mistakes.

For example, in teaching the concept "here and there," if you zoom in to the location identified as "there," "there" may look more like "here."

The following is an example of an unexpected literal interpretation of a video model. For years William had been aversive to music. He would not tolerate our listening to any sort of music at home or in the car, so I thought I would make a video to overcome this problem. I first modeled how to turn on the cassette tape player, then, I moved my hand in front of the camcorder lens while the song played, so that he would be watching a blank screen and would theoretically only absorb the auditory input. Take a guess at what he did. If you guessed that he went over to the player, turned it on, proceeded to cover his eyes with one hand, and listened to the song, you're right. He learned to listen to music, but he also picked up the detail of covering the lens cap by covering his eyes. Needless to say, I made numerous more videos, which included background music. These videos really helped William to tolerate music better.

William's cousin, Kadri, who visited with us in the summer of 2000 from Estonia inadvertently provided William with the practice time he needed with listening to music. Being a teenager, she liked to listen to music – all of the time. Although she spoke English fairly well, she didn't always understand exactly what William was saying to her. For a week or two, William would tell her or would tell someone to tell her to turn it off. She wouldn't, so he just had to continue to listen. Now, he asks for music at home and in the car. We have to smile and thank Kadri when he asks for music.

- Speak slowly and clearly. Introduce new words and unfamiliar voices gradually as your child progresses. A good rule of thumb is to use approximately double the number of words in a phrase or sentence as your child uses spontaneously. For example, if your child talks or comprehends three word sentences, talk in three to six word sentences. Be careful not to pare your language down so much so that your child is in a virtually silent environment. Being around *talking people* is essential to learning how to talk.

- As children with autism are often visual learners, it is important that your actors draw attention to the visual aspect of the lesson. For example, if you are teaching articulation, the actor must be clearly expressive in producing the different sounds. A ventriloquist or actor who talks without moving his lips is not suitable for this lesson.

- Make sure all actors follow your directions (tell them to speak clearly, limit words, etc.). If you're uncomfortable with telling an actor what to say, you could give your actor a written script. Collaborating on video modeling lessons can sometimes yield a better video. If an actor objects to your instructions, he is probably not the right person for the job. You can, of course, always videotape over the audio portion. This may be accomplished by videotaping your video model while it is playing on the VCR with the volume off. As you are videotaping, record your own audio piece.

- Remind actors to be lively and animated when appropriate. The more captivating the videos are, the more your child will gain from them. For example, if you are teaching the pretend play skill of being a doctor, when getting a shot, emphasize the "ouch" and rub the spot where the shot was given. William loved pretending to give shots after this video. If you think your child will learn to be afraid of shots from the "ouch" response, emphasize something else.

- Practice the script with your actors before videotaping. This way you'll know, in advance, if you need to revise the script. Practice as many times as you need, so that you don't make a mistake or inadvertently laugh in the middle of a skit. You will be amazed at how much fun you can have trying to videotape the simplest dialogues. Your bloopers will be fun to watch in years to come – save them!

- Monitor which role your child with autism assumes: the role of the cameraman or the role of the actor. In our case, after William has watched a new video a handful of times, he usually takes the role of the person who is videotaping. The camcorder essentially functions as his eyes and ears. Therefore, when we act, the person who is videotaping plays the role of *William*. The cameraman would respond as though he or she is *William*. And the actor would address the cameraman as *William*.

- As the *producer*, do not eliminate the practice time or reward without keeping good data on the child's progress. You may find, through data collection, that by eliminating either of these parts of the video modeling process, the child may not learn as well.

- If you are acting out a multi-step activity, make sure you talk slowly and present each aspect of the activity clearly. For example, if you are talking about eating, clearly say "First, I get some food on my fork" and model this. Wait a few seconds. Then say, "Then, I put the food in my mouth" and model this. Again, wait for a few seconds before you go on to the next step. Then say, "I chew" and model this. Wait again. Continue on with all the steps involved in eating. Make sure you break down the activity into as many steps as your child needs. For instance, if he is getting the food to his mouth, but is not putting the fork down on the plate, add that as a step.

- For the purpose of drawing your child's attention to the video, you can use voice modulation. William enjoys and is quite fluent at imitating voices of characters in movies. Of course, the intent is not to encourage your child to talk like a cartoon character, but if it helps to make the videos more interesting, it may be worth a try – especially during the reward.

- Have fun! If your child can sense from the tone in your voice and the expression on your faces that you are enjoying this, he will more likely enjoy learning from you.

WRITING THE SCRIPTS: The script is simply a description of the lesson you want to teach, followed by a description of the scene you plan to use to hold your child's attention to the video (the reinforcer or reward).

- As needed, write a short script before you start videotaping. This way you will have a guideline to follow as you go along as well as a record and place to collect data. The scripts can be as short, long, or descriptive as is necessary.

Sample Script

Lesson: Yes/No Questions
> Actor #1:   "Do you want a candy (holding up a candy)?"
> Actor #2 (cameraman): "Yes."
> Actor #1: (Throws a candy to the cameraman).
> Actor #1:   "Do you want a candy (holding up a candy)?"
> Actor #2 (cameraman): "No."
> Actor #1: (Continues to hold the candy)
> * Repeat "yes" and "no" scenario two to three more times

Practice Time with Parent or Teacher to Reinforce Lesson (optional during the video)

Reward or Reinforcer: Play with trains, zoom in on accessories, talk about them going up the hill, through the tunnel, falling off the track, putting them back on the track. Alternate example: Play with dolls. Put the doll in the stroller & take for a walk, dress the doll, put the doll to bed, etc.

- Write your scripts for your programs receptively and expressively, where appropriate. By receptively, it is meant that you are asking your child to show that he understands the question by pointing or gesturing. By expressively, it is meant that you expect your child to provide a verbal response.

- As some children have an exceptional ability to memorize videos, think carefully about the wording you choose for your scripts. If your child has memorized the video and can repeat it verbatim, it's definitely time for a new video. If your child is echolalic with the video modeling scripts, this is an opportunity to interrupt the echolalia. If it's a question and answer video, when your child starts to echo the question, you can fill in the answer and vice versa. For example, if the question is "What is this?" and the answer is "A banana," when your child echoes the question for the second time, you can respond "A banana." Hopefully, this will encourage further interactions and perhaps even develop the skill of asking questions.

- Adjust the length of the lesson and reward to your child's attention span. Start with a one-minute lesson or single activity lesson, if necessary. One minute is not a typo. You will be rewinding and replaying more frequently, but once your child shows an interest in video modeling, you can increase the length of the lesson slowly.

- Watch your child watching the videos. This will be very important in determining which parts are too long, too short, boring or extremely exciting. You can then adjust your scripts accordingly.

VIDEOTAPING THE LESSON: This is what you plan to teach.

- Start with materials and people in your house or classroom, using materials that are easily accessible to your child. If familiar or comfort items from home are included in the school videos and vice versa, the child may be more willing to attend and learn.

- It may be helpful to start video modeling with a very simple lesson, perhaps even of mastered skills. By allowing the child to be successful right from the start, you will build your child's confidence in learning from the video medium.

- It is important to teach the basics first and then the more advanced skills. For example, with video modeling it may be easy to teach a child to recognize a word or read; however, if the child doesn't know the alphabet, it would be more appropriate to teach the individual letters first.

- If after you have had a handful of successes with video modeling you find that your child is not able to demonstrate an understanding of the lesson, try presenting the lesson in another manner or try paring it down. You may have unintentionally stepped up the pace too quickly. Sometimes a small change can make a big difference. For example, if you name ten objects, 20 numbers, and the entire alphabet, try limiting the amount of new material. Redo the video with four objects, five numbers, and a third of the alphabet. If this is still too much, try limiting the number of activities to objects and numbers. Or if you videotaped a simple dialogue involving two actors talking to each other, try zooming in on one actor and assume the role of the other actor yourself while you are videotaping.

- If your child inadvertently learned something inappropriate, it may take quite a bit of undoing. The most effective way is to revideo the same activity without the inappropriate part. You may need to do this several times with stronger reinforcer scenes, so that the original one is a less intense memory. For example, one day back in 1997, I thought I could videotape with William in the house. Right in the middle of a preposition program, William walked into the room, tugged at me and mumbled something when he couldn't get my attention. A few days later, after having watched the video a number of times, he took the train and started practicing the prepositions. He went into the kitchen, held the train *on* the table and said "Where is the train? *on* the table." Then, he held the train *under* the table and said "Where is the train, (mumbled something), *under* the table." I had to film trains *on* and *under* tables a number of times without any extraneous noises, so that he wouldn't practice the mumbling background noise.

- If you are trying to change an existing behavior, recreate the situation that causes the child to behave inappropriately, making sure that your actor acts out the appropriate behavior as a response to the situation. As the ease with which children learn to imitate from videos is one of the reasons video modeling is so successful, it is important never to model behaviors you do not want imitated. If you videotape your actor engaging in a behavior you are trying to eliminate and then videotape your actor engaging in the appropriate behavior, your child may learn to imitate both. They may be paired. Your child may decide that as a matter of routine before I engage in appropriate behavior, I have to misbehave.

For example, if your child screams when other children take toys away from him, the video model might look something like this. You, as cameraman, pretend to be playing with a toy(s). Your actor approaches you and takes your toy away (you do not scream). You say, "Give it back, please" or gesture by putting out your hand. Your actor then returns the toy to you.

In the real world, another child may not necessarily comply as readily as your video modeling actor. So, if your child is still having trouble, you could model the situation in such a way that the child is getting up and going to ask for help.

- You can also use video modeling to tell stories about social situations. This often takes less time than taking photographs, writing a story, and presenting it as a *book*. However, if you have written a *book*, you can also videotape the *book* to reinforce the understanding.

- In the lesson, vary the programs you present and the order in which you present the programs in the video model. If you do not, your child may figure out that you always include a particular lesson first, such as naming objects, and may then elect to tune out until that question and answer format is over.

- It is important to teach your child the meaning of words discretely. In other words, try not to videotape a string of commands your child does not already understand separately. For example, if you are videotaping a how to go to the restaurant skit, unless your child already understands the meaning of "*Let's open the door,*" it may be difficult for your child to understand the expression "*Let's open the door and wait in line.*"

- Generally, the first lesson is the most effective. Always put the most important lesson first. In this way, you have control over whether or not your child is able to turn the television off in an attempt to avoid learning. Once the important lesson has played, your child will likely enjoy continuing to watch, as the reward part of the video gets closer.

- As a general rule, watching the video between 5-10 times should be enough times to affect a change in behavior. If the child is not learning, then the teaching (the video) needs to be modified. Careful observation of the child's reaction to the video will help identify whether fine-tuning or a wholly different approach is necessary.

- If your child is echolalic (repeating words or phrases in place of responsive language) and repeats the scripts over and over again, try making more videos. William went through a period like this. Once he started reciting a script, he had to go through most of it. We were alarmed at first, but decided to keep making more and more videos, thinking that eventually he would hit a saturation point for being able to memorize scripts, especially scripts from long ago. Although he goes through periods of reciting scripts, we can now easily pull him out of scripts, join him in scripts, and generalize the scripts. For example, just recently at a dental appointment for his brother, Erik, William started to explain the visit to Erik and the hygienist in the same words that he remembered from a video model that we made for him over three years ago. As he giggled and talked them through the process, we inserted questions (expecting and coaching his responses) and encouraged him to vary his description of the procedures. He was not locked into running the old script through from start to finish. Rattling off old scripts without having seen them in years, further attests to the power of video modeling and the exceptional memory some children with autism have.

- Use verbal cues to introduce lessons. For example, if you videotape yourself saying, "It's time for your presentation" before you model a presentation, this may be the only prompt your child needs to engage in the activity.

BUILDING IN PRACTICE TIME: This is time built into the video modeling activity for practicing the lesson. For some children, practice time between the lesson and reward can significantly increase the rate of learning.

- There are a number of ways to include practice time. They are described in the following examples.

DURING THE LESSON: The first method involves pausing and practicing as the video plays. For example, while videotaping, ask the question "What is this?" and respond "A banana." Then repeat the question and answer. Make sure to leave a few second pause between the questions to allow enough time for you to locate the pause button on the videocassette recorder or remote. When you play the video for your child, as the question comes up for the second time, push pause, and either wait or help your child to give the right answer. Then let the video continue until the next question appears for the second time. Again, push pause and wait for your child to give a response.

BETWEEN THE LESSON AND REWARD: Alternatively, you can practice for a period of time between the lesson and reward featured on the video. If you choose to build in a five minute practice break, simply videotape the word "work" for five minutes and then, videotape the reward. During the practice time, practice the lesson as it was done on video even in the same order, if necessary. Once your child has memorized the lesson, you can vary the order. If you do not regularly sit down to practice during the five minute practice session every time, your child will probably expect you to fast forward through it. It is important to be consistent right from the beginning. You can also videotape the word work for ten seconds and just keep the video in pause mode until you are finished practicing.

AFTER THE VIDEO: Thirdly, you can practice at the end of the video, after both the lesson and reward have played. At this point, you can motivate your child to practice by withholding the tangibles featured in the reward part of the video until the child has practiced the lesson.

- If you opt not to include practice time as part of the video modeling time, then it is important to practice or quiz your child periodically throughout the day. We try to work the quizzing in as noted in the examples and into our normal routines. For example, when you go shopping your child could practice counting money or help find grocery items. As another example, if you are teaching one-to-one correspondence you could drop bath toys, slowly one by one into the tub, and wait for your child to count or prompt him to count 1-2-3. If you videotaped the lesson in the same fun manner, it will likely be more successful. Be careful, however, you may unwittingly tempt your child into going into the bathtub to practice one-to-one correspondence on his own, without adult supervision.

- If your child is accustomed to watching videos without interruption, it may be difficult for your child to accept being interrupted. Whichever method you choose, it would be better to be consistent and only allow video watching in this manner. You will need to observe your child to decide which method of practicing is more suitable. Remember, if you are *consistent*, this makes it *predictable* for your child.

- The key is to practice at some point so that you know if the video was successful in teaching the lesson. If you were not successful, you may want to present the material in a different manner.

- Accept approximations. If you are waiting for your child to give the correct response to a question, slowly expect improvement in his ability to be able to respond perfectly. For example, if the response you are waiting for is to say "O," and he can only form an "O" with his lips, but cannot get out the sound, accept this and let the video continue. With each successive viewing of the video, expect a closer approximation to the goal, in this case to say "O." After he is able to form an "O" with his lips with ease, the next approximation may be to expect *a sound* with his mouth in an "O" form.

VIDEOTAPING THE REWARD OR REINFORCER: This is the scene your child is waiting for. In order to be effective, it primarily needs to include an activity that is enjoyable and fascinating to him, whether it is functional or not. For some children this may be an activity that involves more work, if they like to work, and for others it may involve play. It essentially reinforces your child's desire to learn by encouraging him to watch the video to the end.

- Adjust the intensity of the reinforcer, as needed. To teach something really difficult or uninteresting, make sure that the reward is especially captivating. If the reinforcer is reinforcing because you are *not* talking, then wait awhile before you add or expand on the language in the reinforcer. Silence may be rewarding for some children.

- If your child seems uninterested or only moderately interested in the reward, tape over the reward. For example, if your child only tunes in when the two toy cars crash into each other, include more crashes. If your child only tunes in when you are feeding the baby doll, feed it more. If your child only tunes in when you empty the dump truck, limit how much of the filling you video and show more dumping. If your child only tunes in when you videotape the ceiling fan going around, then videotape the ceiling fan going around for the reward.

- In the beginning, keep the reinforcer simple. As you are more skilled, use the reinforcer to further develop language and skills. For example, if you are teaching prepositions (on, in, under, behind, next to, in front, etc.) then emphasize the prepositions in the reinforcer. You can do this by talking through your reinforcer. If you are using play with a doll, you could say, "Look, the baby doll is walking *behind* the sofa. Now look, the doll is sitting *on* Mommy's lap."

- If your child is getting tired with a particular type of reward, such as play with dolls, but also has restricted interests, vary the things you do with the preferred toys. You could go to a doll museum or take the doll for a walk outside in the stroller and add that to the end of the lesson. If train play is getting boring, go to a train museum, train show or a train garden.

- If your child's interests are limited to the non-functional, start by using these activities in the reward scenes and gradually *develop interest in more functional activities.* If spinning a top and watching it until it falls, over and over, is reinforcing to your child, then it is reasonable to use this activity in the reward. However, keep in mind that video modeling encourages imitation when choosing the reward scene.

- In order to expand on the child's repertoire of reinforcing activities, you could try videotaping two simultaneous activities in the reward scene. On one side of the screen you would have a spinning top, on the other side of the screen you would have something similar, but more adaptable, such as an airplane mobile. You could just blow on the mobile ever so slightly to give it some motion. If your child starts to show interest in the airplane mobile, eventually you might be able to develop some pretend airplane play. If your child wants to throw away the airplane mobile, then you might try pasting an airplane on the top and let it spin around. Just keep trying!

- Children with autism often have difficulty with the unexpected and unpredictable. When videotaping, you may inadvertently model something that is totally unforeseen for your child. This may cause an emotional reaction. We have inadvertently videotaped reward scenes that have caused a surge of emotions in our son. The first time a toy train accidentally rode off the track and brought down 10 coaches with it, William didn't know whether to cry or laugh. He wanted the video off, then on, then off, then on. Eventually, he got used to it and started crashing them himself. The accidental train crash had an unintended, beneficial effect. He no longer tries to stop his peers from crashing toy cars and wooden trains. On the other hand, we have also had to send numerous electric model trains back to the manufacturer for repair work.

- Another option may be to seek out permission, if necessary, from a commercial video licensor to copy a brief part of one of your child's favorite videos to add to the end of your educational video.

- As an alternative, you could just film a video case to let your child know that at the end of the lesson, you will switch videos and put in a favorite video.

- Some children enjoy looking through the viewfinder or LCD display. By supporting and guiding the camera, while the child is holding it, you can record the reward that they are seeking to view.

- Do not use inappropriate reinforcing activities that may be harmful or embarrassing to your child (for example, self-injurious behavior).

- Some children, being masters of behavior management, are overly rewarded throughout the course of daily living. In order for video modeling or any other method to be effective, the reward for learning needs to be greater. This can be accomplished by paring back the rewards that are available to the child on a daily basis.

VIEWING THE VIDEO WITH YOUR CHILD: This is an opportunity to see if you were successful in teaching the lesson.

- Before you show the video to your child, watch it yourself to make sure there are no mistakes and to minimize unintended effects.

- If your child completely tunes out the lesson right from the start, stop the video, fast forward to just before the reward and then push play again. With each successive viewing, rewind to a point just before the last time. This is also known as *backward chaining.*

- In the beginning, until your child shows an interest in video modeling, you may need to put away his favorite videos.   In some children, this may elicit a tantrum. We were able to successfully put away all of William's favorite videos.   When he asked for his favorite video, we would simply say, "Look, this is all there is (and show him the empty shelf)." If this seems too difficult because you know your child will make you miserable if you say no and you don't want to be increasingly miserable before it gets better (also known as the *extinction burst*), you could try telling him "First, watch this *new* (with emphasis and enthusiasm) video, then you can watch your favorite video." You will know if your reward was successful because your child will opt to watch the video model over his favorite video. Some children instinctively ask for "The Mommy Video," having recognized the voice and giving the video a name.

- Many of the new camcorders have a wonderful added feature called a liquid crystal display (LCD) screen.   This allows you to replay the recorded video on a small screen built into the camera. If you have this type of camcorder, you may be able to use *instant replay* to teach. For instance, if your child becomes anxious about a particular activity, if you have assistance, you or your helper could videotape the activity without him, and play it back on the LCD screen. Instantly, your child would see that the activity is somewhat predictable. Your child may then be able to understand that there is nothing to fear and will be able to participate in the activity.

While we didn't use video modeling on the spot in this example, we did preview an event for William, so that we could manage his anxiety. For William's 7th birthday, we planned a party for him at the B & O Railroad Museum. There would be cake in the dining car, a museum visit, and a train ride. Although we knew that he would love the museum, we also knew that he might have difficulty being on and near the real trains. Therefore, we decided to go to the museum the weekend before for a trial run to capture as much as we could on video so that we could use video modeling to get him to be more comfortable with the museum activities. I was expecting to walk and talk while videotaping the train ride alone. William surprised us by boarding the train. So, I videotaped William from behind, getting on the train, walking to his seat, and *somewhat* enjoying the ride. The conductor said, "You're getting a real nice shot of the back of his head!" I am sure the conductor questioned my videotaping skills. He had no idea that William was strategically positioned between Dad (leader) and Mom (follower). We knew that William was more likely to follow Dad on to the train. If I was in front of William, he may have panicked, run off, and there wouldn't have been a video to watch that included William as a part of the activity. We watched the video during the week before his party. The party was a complete success.

- In the beginning, do not be overly concerned if your child does not sit down to watch the video from start to finish. If he is walking around the room, he may be memorizing the content of the video. Some of us need to pace while learning. At a minimum, the child is being rewarded for checking in with the video from time to time. If you decide to stop the video and only play the video if the child is sitting and watching, the child may decide to only watch videos for which there is a really terrific reward at the end. Both methods of permitting video viewing have their advantages and disadvantages. The manner, in which you decide to reinforce the lesson, depends largely on you and your understanding of the needs of your child.

- While you are viewing the video with your child, you can use the volume control to gain and maintain the child's attention to the video. By raising the volume, the audio feed gets louder, but it doesn't sound like the actors are screaming. In working one-to-one with some children, it can be difficult to modulate your voice without causing the children to get confused. For some children, a word spoken in a whisper is a different word.

- With children with autism, the continuous observation of whether or not teaching is causing learning to occur is of the utmost importance.

SPECIFIC TIPS AND EXAMPLES ON HOW TO VIDEO

The following tips and examples on how to videotape is a sampling of different approaches to a variety of activities.

ACTIONS. Actions include waving, jumping, sneezing, running, walking, coughing, laughing, etc. The standard question and answer format is "Q: What is (he) doing? A: (action)." Start by videotaping your actor modeling an action. Then ask, "What is (he) doing?" When modeling actions receptively, ask your actor to "show me (action)." This can be very entertaining. If your child is imitating an exaggerated response, you may need to revideo the actions with less enthusiasm, using a powerful reinforcer to try to diminish the memory of prior videos. You can also just give the command for the action such as *jump* instead of *show me jumping* and then show your actor jumping. This is one of my favorites - when I ask someone to jump and they jump!

ALPHABET. When teaching letters, zoom in on one letter at a time or point to the target letter. While recording, provide the question and answer "Q: What letter is this? A: (letter)." Don't videotape the entire alphabet in one video; break it down into logical groups, A-G for example, or if this is too much then A-C. Once your child knows the alphabet, you can record yourself mixing up the letters and putting them in order. You can also point to the letters and sing the alphabet song.

APPROPRIATE PLAY. There are many aspects of appropriate play to teach. I think it is helpful to start in the home environment with familiar toys that are accessible to your child. If the school setting is set up for play, then certainly appropriate play can be video modeled there as well. The following examples illustrate some of the ways that you can encourage the development of play skills.

I videotaped myself playing with William's wooden train set, videotaping with one hand and maneuvering the trains with the other. I talked about what I was doing and which engines were doing what. William doesn't line them up anymore. He quickly switched to playing with them just as he has seen me do on video and even started to invite me to join him. Now that he has a repertoire of what to do with his train sets, he has begun to improvise on his own. He loves to recreate crash and disaster scenes. While to an outsider it may look reckless, it is pretend play.

To expand on his interest in toys, I videotaped play with a toy castle and knight set, which he previously had no interest in. I had the dragon try to get in the castle and let the knights fire cannonballs at the dragon until he retreated. William will now engage in this game with me.

If your child wanders on the playground, seemingly uninterested in playground equipment, you can either videotape as you slide and swing or you can ask someone to videotape you. Videotaping with one hand and engaging in an activity involving movement can be challenging.

ART PROJECTS. In this type of lesson, you are building on the pre-academic skills of cutting, gluing, pasting, and coloring. Start off by introducing the activity. For example, say, "Let's draw a picture of the family." Then, videotape as you draw each family member. You can also model writing their names under their pictures. William learned to draw some simple pictures this way.

ARTICULATION OR PRONUNCIATION. Zoom in on the mouth of your actor. It may seem unusual at first, but it is an effective way to focus your child's attention to the articulation or imitation of sounds. Press RECORD and slowly say "Say (a sound or word)." Wait for your actor to respond (in advance, remind them to speak slowly and very clearly). Then continue on with more sounds or words in the same manner. If your child is still not able to imitate sounds, slow them down and stretch them out even more. For example, the word "mommy" which normally takes one second to say could be stretched to "mmmmm (3 seconds) oooooo (3 seconds) mmmmm (3 seconds) eeeee (3 seconds)." Some sounds lend themselves to being stretched more than others.

ATTENTION. Focus the camcorder on your actor. Tell him "Look at me." Make sure your actor knows to look directly at the camcorder for a few seconds or as long as you feel your child would be able to tolerate. It is important to keep in mind the normal limits of attention and eye contact. Think about how long you would feel comfortable sustaining eye contact or attending to a person before you move. You can tell your actor "Good job" or give him a food item, such as a small candy, that your child with autism likes. Once your child has seen the video five times, try telling him "Look at me." If he responds appropriately, make sure you provide the praise ("Good job" or the food item he saw on the video model). If he still is not responding to the command "Look at me," try showing the video another five times or modify the way you present the command. This may include reversing roles between the cameraman and actor. The actor would say, "Look at me" and the cameraman would turn in the direction of the actor.

BATHING. This is a very sensitive activity to videotape. Do not videotape your child or actor in such a way that would be embarrassing if another person, adult or child were to see the video while it is being replayed over and over in order to teach the skill. If you have a cooperative actor, you can let them say, "First, I wash my hair," showing them going through the steps involved in hair washing (wetting your hair, getting the shampoo, putting a small amount in the palm of your hand, rubbing your hands together, then washing your hair). Wait a few seconds and then let your actor continue, "Then, I wash myself," showing the steps involved (washing both arms, chest – for boys and men – and legs from the knees to the toes, etc.). As your child becomes familiar with bathing you can also teach him how to turn on the water, adjust the temperature, what level to fill the tub to, how to turn off the water, how to towel dry, etc.

COINS & CURRENCY. In this lesson, you can teach the value of coins and currency, addition with money, and how to pay for things at the check out counter. You may be able to find a store manager that will go along with your video modeling request. They may even let you stand at a closed register to videotape pretend shopping. If not, you can always use a pretend cash register and an actor, to play the part of the store clerk, at home.

In our case, we opted to take photos of the steps involved in going to the toy store and from the photos created a simple story to read while we videotaped. This helped William to understand that he had to wait in line to pay before he could go.

COLORS. Teach three to four new colors at a time. If this is too much, teach even less in each new video. Use the question and answer format

"Q: What color is this? A: (color)." Once your child knows the basic colors (red, blue, green, yellow, brown, pink, gray, black, white, orange, purple), you can start identifying familiar objects by their color. So, if your child can identify the object, car for example, the next step would be to ask him "Q: What color is the (object)? A: The (object) is (color)."

CUTTING, GLUING, PASTING, COLORING. For these activities you may need help. You may want to zoom in on the hands of your actor, so that you minimize distracting items. Videotape over your actor's shoulder so that the video is presented in the same manner that the child will be expected to practice. The mirror image factor (left to right reversal) can be eliminated and the perspective will be clearer. Present each activity separately, so that there is no confusion about what cut, glue, paste and color mean. Once your child understands the meaning of these words, then you can more successfully videotape a complex activity.

DRESSING. People may be a little hesitant to helping with a dressing video. Snapping, buttoning, and tying shoes can be modeled easily by describing what you are doing – push, pull through, cross the lace.

For the actual dressing routine you could try something like this: start videotaping and say "First I get my clothes (walk over to the dresser, open it, identify the clothing items you are taking out, and set them on the bed), then I put on my shirt" (push pause and call in someone to help film while you dress a child, preferably your child – you will need to do this on a day when your child is being cooperative). Put the shirt on your child and make sure the person who is videotaping understands that he is only to videotape the child's chest (if you are dressing a girl, you should not videotape her chest – you may need to show her putting on a shirt over a shirt). Then say, "Then I put on my underpants (do not film your child without clothing on – the person who is videotaping should be instructed to videotape the underpants going on his ankles only). Pull up the underpants with the camcorder on pause (do not show your child in underpants on video because if anyone else sees the video, particularly children, they will probably embarrass your child). Then say, "Then I pull up my pants (here again, only show the pants going on the ankles)." Then show the child fully dressed, and finally you can give him a reward (a candy, token, sticker, etc.).

As you practice dressing, the steps that were not modeled on video will be taught as part of the sequence. I have found that some children with autism can naturally problem solve the missing step. You can continue on with socks and shoes and other articles of clothing as the seasons change. After your child has had the opportunity to watch the dressing video a number of times, offer him the opportunity to dress himself and be sure to provide the same reward that he saw on the video.

EATING A MEAL. This can be broken down into many single videos – setting the table, eating, socializing, clearing the table. Again, videotape as you talk through the steps of setting the table, sitting down, waiting for the food to be served, eating (yes, you can get a bite on your fork, bring the fork to your mouth, set the fork on your plate, chew and videotape at the same time), then continue with being finished, saying thank you, and clearing your plate to the kitchen.

I once made a video for a friend to model *finishing all the food on the plate*. I enlisted the help of my son, so that the video would be modeled from both perspectives. We each had four pieces of rigatoni pasta on our plates. As I videotaped we took turns eating our respective food. After each bite, not wanting to talk with food in my mouth, discretely I flung the pasta off the fork behind me while I continued to record. Needless to say, my son was amused to see his mother behave this way while we were videotaping.

EMOTIONS. Emotions include happy, sad, mad, scared, surprised, guilty, etc. This can be a very funny lesson to videotape. You will need to videotape yourself or find a cooperative actor to show various emotions. If you are videotaping yourself, you will need to set the camcorder on a table or tripod, push RECORD, sit in the area where the camcorder is directed, tell yourself

"Show me (emotion)," and exaggerate the emotion. You can also give the verbal cue from out of view. Then, pop into the field and display the emotion. It is a good idea to rewind and replay scenes of yourself, videotaped by yourself, to make sure you are actually in the picture. Be careful not to accidentally laugh while you are videotaping because your child will probably laugh too, even if it doesn't correspond with the emotion.

ENVIRONMENTAL SOUNDS. Environmental sounds include the sound of footsteps, a kettle whistling, the doorbell, a fire engine, etc. The standard question and answer format is "Q: What do you hear? A: I hear a (object that is making the sound)." For example, you could let the kettle whistle and ask, "What do you hear?" The answer is "I hear a kettle." This is a good example of an activity that could be potentially dangerous if your child decides to turn the stove on without adult supervision to recreate an opportunity to practice. Some other suggestions that are easy to video are a car honking and toys with animal sounds. While asking the question, keep the camcorder focused on a blank wall. Then, when you disclose the answer you can video the object. This may help to develop auditory processing.

FEARS. When creating a video model to overcome a fear, it is important not to show the state of being fearful. In other words, you do not want to demonstrate being fearful and demonstrate not being fearful. Use the tone of your voice to assure that everything is all right as you walk and talk your way through the activity that is causing the fear.

In our case, William was petrified of most animals and flying insects. Not knowing how frightened William would be, the special education team decided to bring a pet rabbit to keep in school. Everything was fine until one of William's classmates accidentally let the rabbit out of the cage. Naturally, it started running around the classroom. Just as expected, the next day William refused to go into the classroom. Once they got him in, he wouldn't put his feet on the floor and couldn't concentrate on his work.

I decided to try making a video to overcome this fear. I videotaped myself opening the rabbit cage and putting my hand in to pet the rabbit; I said "Nice bunny" as I continued to pet the rabbit. I also showed myself touching the outside of the cage. After William watched the video for a few days, I decided to try bringing him in to see the rabbit. He didn't like the idea, but he went along with it. The rabbit had been moved to another part of the building, so it was a little less scary. I put my hand in the cage, pet the rabbit, and said "Nice bunny." Then I said, "It's your turn, then we go." William put his hand in the cage, pet the rabbit, said "Nice bunny," and then we left. The special educator that was teaching a class in the room was astonished. As I was walking out the door, she said, "This is a book."

Since then we have also addressed his dog fear. We did a similar video with my in-laws' puppy. Again, it worked surprisingly well; we were able to have dinner with them again. However, the puppy grew into a jumpy poodle. After seeing William's reaction to the hyper dog, we made another video, which again worked well.

Then, we decided to get our own dog. Not having had a dog to practice the skills he had learned on the previous videos, we were almost back to square one again. So, one night after William had fallen asleep on the sofa, we brought out the camcorder. I set the dog on the blanket that was covering William; he didn't startle. We proceeded to videotape William sleeping with the dog resting on top of him. When we showed him the video the next day, he was truly surprised. We were more surprised when he pulled the same blanket over himself and asked us to put the dog on him.

Flying animals and insects are more difficult to videotape. I videotaped birds chirping in trees, which helped. When I found a baby bird in a nest that was also learning how to fly, I knew I had a winner. I was able to get very close and let William see the bird jumping from tree limb to tree limb. The zoom of the camcorder gave the appearance that I was within inches of the bird. He very willingly came outside and went right to the bush to find the bird.

FUNCTIONS OF OBJECTS. In this lesson, you are basically asking the question "what do you do with a (object)," while holding the object. When giving the answer, it may be helpful to demonstrate the action also. For example, if the question is "What do you do with a pencil," you could answer, "I write with a pencil," while simultaneously writing with the pencil. Some other suggestions for broad categories of functions of objects include the following:

1   Q: What do you do with a (food items)?
    A: I eat (food items).
2   Q: What do you do with (drink items)?
    A: I drink (drink items).
3   Q: What do you do with (toy items)?
    A: I play with (toy items).
4   Q: What do you do with (clothing items)?
    A: I wear (clothing items).
5   Q: What do you do with (vehicular items)?
    A: I ride in (vehicular items).

There are many different ways to teach this concept. The more you model, the greater the likelihood that the concept will be generalized.

GOING PLACES. Video modeling is a good way to introduce how to go to a new place or overcome a fear of going to a particular place. If it is impractical to actually go through the motions of going to a restaurant, a movie, the grocery store, etc., the next best thing is to take pictures and make a little storybook. Then, you can read the storybook on video and bring the book along *to the place*, so that you have a visual aid to follow while you are at the restaurant, movie, grocery store, etc.

GREETINGS. The first step is to teach your child to shake hands and say "Hi." Shaking hands is simple. While videotaping, let your actor extend his hand toward you, then focus the camcorder on the hands approaching each other, and then capture the handshake. You can then re-focus the camera to the face of your actor, at which point, your actor will say, "Hi (name of your child)." You would then respond back "Hi."

GROOMING. To videotape grooming, you will need to give a command and then show the grooming skill. For example, give the command "Brush your teeth" and then zoom in on the mouth of your actor and show how he is brushing all the surfaces. Thoroughness may need to be practiced over time. This applies to most children.

HANDS DOWN OR HANDS QUIET. If your child has overly sensitive hearing and frequently covers his ears, videotaping can help model what (put your) *hands down or hands quiet* means. If the dishwasher is too loud, you could videotape one of your actors standing next to a running dishwasher with his hands covering his ears. Your actor could say, "It's too loud." Then, you could turn off the dishwasher and say "Put your hands down." Your actor would then put down his hands and show a feeling of relief on his face. You can do a similar video with a hair dryer, loud music, and other noises that you have control over that are bothersome. If your child cannot possibly have control over the noises, you can model on video how to say, "It's too loud, I need to go."

IDENTIFYING ROOMS. As you enter a room, videotape the threshold, cross the threshold, then focus on the room and ask, "What room is this?" Then, provide the answer.

MANNERS. These appear in many of the lessons. It is important to emphasize manners, such as please and thank you, so that they are not overlooked. Sometimes a visual cue is helpful.

If your child can already adequately make his needs and wants known (requesting), but doesn't say please, you can make a flash card with the word please on it, pop the flash card in front of the lens of the camcorder, at the appropriate moment, and simultaneously say please after your request. Keep the flash card in your pocket, so that if your child forgets to say please, you can pop the flash card in front of him as a quick reminder.

In order to video model *thank you*, you can videotape your actor giving you something. Your actor would not release the object to you until you say *thank you*.

MATCHING. There are all sorts of matching lessons you can write up and video. If you have taught sight word recognition for the colors, you can match the color with the color word by drawing a line to connect them. You can do an identical picture-to-picture match. You can match objects that go together (pencil-paper, fork-spoon, toothpaste-toothbrush, blanket-bed, key-door, etc.). At the beginning of the video say, "Match." Then do the activity. If you can talk your way through the lesson, that may be helpful. For instance, first say, "Match," then say, "Pencil goes with paper, fork goes with spoon, etc." as you draw the line or move the object or photo.

MATH. Use manipulatives or visual aids, such as small blocks or candies. If you are teaching addition, put the manipulatives under the numbers on a piece of paper. For example, on a piece of paper write 1+1=2 in large print. Then, put one block under each number one. After you have read "1+1," then push the two blocks under the number two and say "=2." Of course, there are many other ways to present this simple math problem. You may need to try several different presentations until you figure out which is the easiest way for your child to understand it. We have used candies to teach counting and addition. At the end of the lesson, I ate the candies on video. William had fun with this because he knew he could eat the lesson!

MUSIC. There are many aspects of music that can be taught on video. You can show how to identify and play simple instruments, how to operate a cassette or CD player and sit down and listen to a song. You can point to the words of a song while it plays, and even teach body movements to music. Keep the camcorder steady and talk clearly.

We also used video modeling to overcome William's over-sensitivity to music and his fear of going to music class in school. The music and physical education teachers helped to make the video. We videotaped three songs. For the first one, we pointed to the words while the song played. For the second one, the music and physical education teachers acted out the movements (witch, frog, horse, fish, and bird). This was one time when all three of us couldn't keep from laughing while I was videotaping. The music muffled our laughing. For the third song, we pointed to the words and the music teacher sang along. I played the video for William for one week before I tried to introduce him to the music room. At first, we went in without the class to listen to one song at a time. After a few days, we all agreed that he was ready to try going with his classmates. I think everyone around was impressed that he stayed for 17 of the 30 minute music lesson on the first day.

To further help William overcome his music sensitivity, I started to include background music during the reward element of the videos. William quickly gained an appreciation for Mozart. He would automatically go and turn on the stereo before turning on the electric trains.

NAMING OBJECTS. Depending on your child's visual memory skill level, adjust the number of objects you model in each videotape. We have found that four to five new items per video seems to be about the limit for William. When videotaping, make sure that there are no other visible objects in the viewfinder, including pictures on the wall or colorful wall paper, otherwise, he may confuse the name of the object with a distracting item. Push RECORD, ask the question, "What is this?" and provide the answer. In the beginning, it may be helpful to repeat the question and answer for each object.

This can also be done by taking a walking tour and commenting on the names of objects without first providing a question stimulus. This may encourage more spontaneous commenting.

NUMBERS. Videotape numbers in logical groups. We started with 1-10, but if this is too much, start with 1-3. The next step would be 10-20 and so on. It is also a good idea to mix them up and put them in order. This will help in understanding what comes after. The typical question and answer format is "Q: What number is this? A: (number)." Here again, zoom in on the target number or point to the number you are talking about.

With our first videos, during the practice time, William used his hands to cover his peripheral vision as he approached the target number. We quickly realized that he was trying to simulate "the zoom" of the video. Over time, he stopped doing this.

OPPOSITES. In this lesson, you will need pairs of opposites (such as big/little, wet/dry, tall/short, etc.). It is important that the items are otherwise identical. Although you can teach them separately, the following example is a reason to teach them together.

William had a habit of constantly asking us to raise or lower the volume on the television. This is something he could clearly do himself if he knew which button to push. I thought it would be easier if I modeled one or the other first – I chose raising the volume. I started with the volume at level 10 and clicked the button ten times to get to level 20. I wanted it to clearly get louder. When William went to practice this new skill, he started at level 20, clicked the button ten times and reached volume *level 30*! It was obvious we needed to quickly teach him the opposite.

PARTS OF BODY. The question and answer format is "Q: What is this? A: (part of body – such as nose, eye, knee)." Once your child has mastered most parts of the body, you can teach him whose (part of body)?" You can also teach him to "Touch your (part of body – such as shoulder, elbow, mouth)." I videotaped an almost life-size photo of my children to teach this lesson. At a younger age, William was always more interested in *big* materials. I videotaped the photo while pointing to and identifying the parts of the body.

PEOPLE. To teach the names of unfamiliar people on video, you can videotape the person or a photo of the person. You can even videotape a video of the person. Simply zoom in on the TV (if you can, pause the VCR while it is displaying the unfamiliar person), the photo or the person and record yourself questioning and answering "Who is this?" (name of person)." If you videotape a photo and then wear the photo of yourself as a necklace, the connection between photo and person may be easier to establish.

As an alternative, you can also name the people without asking a question. The advantage to providing the question stimulus is that the child has memorized a cue to the information that is being asked for.

PHYSICAL EDUCATION ACTIVITIES. If you can go through the motions of the activity from the child's perspective, the video will probably be more successful. For instance, if you are teaching tag, hold the camcorder steady and pretend to chase your actor very slowly, then tag him and say, "You're it." Then, show the actor turning around and running toward you, run away slowly, always holding the camcorder steady, for five to ten seconds. Then, let your actor tag you. You can point the camcorder to your arm, so that you can show yourself being tagged. After your actor says, "You're it," turn around and repeat the game. At first, play an artificially slow game, so that it is easier to follow.

Sometimes, the child's perspective is impossible to videotape. An example is jumping jacks. As jumping jacks are a complex series of motor movements, for all children, we decided to videotape our actor going through the steps of putting a jumping jack together. For our jumping jack video, sequentially we videotaped the following. First, we videotaped *feet apart, feet together*. Then, we videotaped *arms up, arms down* zooming in on the action. Then, we videotaped *feet apart, arms up* and *feet together, arms down*, which gave us one jumping jack. Each separate step was videotaped three or four times. Then, we videotaped a series of three jumping jacks, still providing the verbal cues described in the earlier steps. The last clip in the jumping jack video was the actor doing a series of jumping jacks to the direction "let's do jumping jacks."

If you are videotaping a sports game, it may be helpful to talk and point your way through the game. For example, if you are videotaping a basketball game, try to follow the ball and talk about which team has *it*. If someone gets it in the net, with enthusiasm say, "That's two points." As sports games involve a lot of movement, pointing by keeping your hand in front of the lens may help to give the child a frame of reference for following the game.

PREPARING FOR MEDICAL PROCEDURES. There are few activities that are as fear provoking as a visit to the doctor or a medical procedure. This fear arises from not being able to *predict* the course of the visit and the fact that the patient has little *control.*

For us, most visits and procedures have been manageable without video modeling intervention. Electrophysiology, however, was not so easy. Our first attempt was fruitless. So, I set up a mock electrophysiology visit at home with William's older brother, Erik, as the actor. I purchased six strands of telephone wire and a package of adhesive putty used to hang children's artwork. For William's benefit, Erik let me videotape him as I pretended to attach leads. The electrophysiologist had shown me the approximate location of the six leads. I proceeded to press six pieces of adhesive putty onto Erik's scalp, and then placed a strand of telephone wire into each. He also had an ear insert in each ear. Once he was wired, Erik had to sit quietly and watch a video (one of William's favorites) for ten minutes while I videotaped. During the actual procedure, William would be able to watch a video. I walked and talked my actor through the mock procedure, always maintaining a calm and confident manner. When William arrived for his next electrophysiology visit, he was compliant.

PRESENTATIONS. Giving a presentation is nothing more than acting, so it is well suited for video modeling. If you have taught your child to respond by imitating a video model, then learning from a mock presentation on video should be relatively easy. Videotape the presentation from both perspectives using cue cards to read from, if necessary. You can include a verbal cue such as "It's time for your presentation" to alert your child that it's his turn.

PRETEND PLAY. All sorts of play can be acted out on video: 1) pretending to be an animal (a cat, a dog, a cow) – you need to get on all fours and make the animal noises, 2) pretending to be a community worker (a policeman, a doctor, a fireman, a trash collector, a mailman) – if you have props your skit will be more convincing, 3) pretending to be a vehicle (a train, an airplane, a race car) – emphasize the body movements and sounds, 4) pretending to go shopping – if you pretend to buy candy, use real money and eat the candy, so that the lesson may be more meaningful.

READING. Reading has many aspects: memorizing sight words, articulation, reading text, story sequencing, answering comprehension questions.

To model sight word recognition, the standard question and answer format is "Q: What does this say? Or what word is this? A: (word)." Once your child is familiar with reading sight words, this becomes a wonderful tool for teaching longer responses. For example, if you are teaching answers to rote questions, such as "how old are you," you can videotape the response while pointing to the words on paper. In the beginning, it may be helpful to use large print. You may also want to use simple fonts, such as Century Gothic, that do not have extraneous curls.

To make sight word recognition a fun activity, I have placed one word on each step on the staircase. As I walked up the steps, I zoomed in on each word as I called it out. I have also used William's fascination with trains to strengthen his sight word vocabulary. While videotaping, I rolled and stopped William's favorite engine at each of approximately ten sight words. At each stop I asked, "What word is this" and provided the answer. I was pleasantly surprised to find William independently setting up the sight word flashcards along side his train and then practicing.

To model reading, you could either set a book on your lap, on a table, or on the floor in front of you. Hold the camcorder in one hand and point to each word with your other hand as you read. Read slowly and clearly. If there is too much text per page, you might try paraphrasing. At first, William expected us to remember the paraphrases, but soon he was showing us that he was remembering the paraphrases himself because his articulation had improved.

After using video modeling to read a bedtime story (I sat in his bed and propped the book on my lap while I videotaped), for the first time,

William brought me a book for us to read before bedtime.

To teach sequencing, you could try the following. If you have a simple story line, start by drawing a picture of the main points of the story. As you read along, put the pictures on the appropriate pages. After you have read the story, sit down at a table and put the pictures in order and paraphrase the story.

REQUESTING. To teach your child how to request, the cameraman pushes RECORD, then says, "I want (object)." Instruct your actor to give you the object. Videotape this with various different objects, so that your child can generalize (appropriately adapt) the "I want" to objects that were not modeled on video. It may take videotaping 5, 10, 50 objects all prefaced by "I want," until your child realizes the meaning of the expression "I want." If you use objects that your child really does want, the video will probably be more meaningful.

RIDING A BIKE AND BRAKING. Riding a bike is a very complex activity. For us, the complexity began before even sitting on the bicycle. It began with a fear of trying something new.

In order to interest William in riding, or even scooting a bicycle forward, we videotaped a scenario in which William's dad rode William's bike from one end of the driveway to the other. We had parked a brand new HO scale steam engine at the opposite end of the driveway. William watched the video a number of times. At first, William headed straight for the reward (the HO scale train). He quickly realized that he would have to get the bicycle from one end of the driveway to the other if he wanted to play with the train.

The next step was peddling. It was modeled, video modeled, and practiced.

Then, we had to get the training wheels off. Again, this was modeled, video modeled, and practiced.

And lastly, once he started riding, we needed to teach him how to stop. In order to teach William how to brake, William's dad rode the bike while I videotaped and I rode the bike while William's dad videotaped. We even placed a red sock on the pedal and demonstrated how to push back, but to no avail. Whether we attempted teaching one-on-one or on video, nothing was effective. He simply couldn't brake. It was easier for William to ride off the street into the gully. He learned to use gravity and friction instead.

Just at about the same time, one of the anchors of the local ABC™ morning news show in Washington, D.C. agreed to do a story on our experience with video modeling. The producers asked if they could take some B roll footage (the family engaged in our normal daily activities). They suggested bike riding. Everything was fine until the cameraman set his $30,000 camera on the driveway to capture William approaching. At the very last second, the cameraman realized that William was not intent on stopping, but rather intent on crashing into the camera. The cameraman picked it up just in time.

This may have been the defining moment where I realized that videotaping from William's perspective might be the answer. So, I told my husband that I was going to ride William's bicycle down our street and videotape at the same time. His response was, "I can't watch this. You are surely going to end up with broken bones and a broken camcorder." I set out on the bicycle. When it was time to stop, I zoomed in on the handbrake and explained what I was doing. What I didn't do was peddle. I was able to alternate footsteps while I rode the bike down the hill to simulate a bike ride, hence no broken bones and no broken camera. William watched the video and learned to brake.

RIDING PUBLIC TRANSPORTATION. This is essentially videotaped in the same manner as GOING PLACES. If there are any fears involved in entering a bus, train, taxicab, or airplane, it may be helpful to see this on video for the purpose of overcoming the fear. Your child will be able to watch the video from a personal perspective and will hopefully realize that there is nothing to fear, especially if he hears a familiar, comforting voice talking their way through the video. If a fear is involved, keep the content matter of fact and the tone of your voice enthusiastic, not anxious.

ROTE CONVERSATION. This is an extension of greetings. If your child can watch a conversation on video and then practice, it may help your child to understand that conversation is an exchange of ideas or opinions, even though his responses may be rote (memorized regardless of meaning). It may be helpful to hold a script and point to the responses you are giving. This way, your child will have a script (a visual cue) to hold, to make it easier to remember the rote responses.

You can teach rote responses for all sorts of standard greetings, such as 1) Hi, what's going on? (Nothing much)) 2) Hi, how are you? (I'm fine) 3) Hi, how's it going? (O.K.) 4) Hey, what's happening? (Not much). There are many ways these very simple greetings arise. The more of them you video, the easier it will be for your child to respond when the question varies slightly.

ROTE QUESTIONS & ANSWERS. Examples include name, address, telephone number and other questions for which the answer is always the same. These are good questions for your child to be able to answer for both social as well as safety reasons. If you videotape a blank wall while asking the question, your child will have to memorize the auditory input. Then, when you give the answer you could offer a visual cue by pointing to the words on a piece of paper as you read them out loud. The visual cue, the answer on a piece of paper, is a prompt. Eventually, you will need to fade the prompt, so that the child can answer without being given any clues.

SAFETY. There are many safety issues that children with autism need to learn. One of the most fundamental issues is being able to identify where you are with a simple "Here I am." This can be accomplished by videotaping an actor hiding behind a diversion. The actor hides and you ask, "(Name of child) where are you?" The actor responds, "Here I am." By varying and repeating the *here I am* scenario several times, it may be easier for the child to generalize the concept. This may be very helpful if your child likes to disappear in the department store clothes racks.

Identifying property boundaries on video may also be helpful. For example, you could videotape a scenario in which you chase a ball to an artificial boundary at which point you go to ask for help in retrieving the ball.

SCIENCE & SOCIAL STUDIES. Any school activity can be pre-taught, even if it is as simple as going through the worksheets. The hands-on activities will probably be the more memorable. You may be able to get permission to videotape in school. In this case, you will probably capture a lot of background noise that will take away from the lesson. To correct this, you can record over the audio part by re-making the video. Simply play the video on your VCR with the volume off and videotape your television with your camcorder. While the video is playing, you can talk through the science & social studies lesson in words your child understands.

SHAPES. Shapes can be worked on in many ways. They can be identified discretely and in the natural surroundings. The standard question and answer format for identifying shapes discretely is "Q: What shape is this? A: (shape)."

SITTING AT A DESK. If sitting at a desk is difficult for your child, push *record* on your camcorder, tell your actor to *sit at your desk,* show your actor sitting properly at his desk for 30-60 seconds, then give him a reward while you are still videotaping (the reward can be a sticker, a token, a small edible, etc.). In the next scene, tell your actor to *keep sitting at your desk*, then show him still sitting properly for another 30-60 seconds, follow with a reward, repeat the cycle of continuing to sit one more time. Once your child can sit for a full three minutes, you could do a new video, which starts with a *sit at your desk command* and is followed by *do your work command.* If your child has trouble with the first 30 seconds of sitting, you could try shortening the time to 5-15 seconds.

SPELLING. If spelling is difficult for your child, there are a number of ways to make this easier with video modeling. You can videotape homework expectations. You can also create a video, which pairs a favorite activity with spelling.

This might involve pairing a letter with a doll or train car to form a word. As long as the activity is enjoyable, you have the ability to develop it.

SURROUNDINGS. The question and answer format is similar to naming objects, "Q: What is this? A: (place or object)." When videotaping surroundings, you can also easily walk around, zooming in on trees, shrubs, decks, the sky, etc., further teaching the names of objects.

TOILETING. If toilet training is difficult for your child or there are problems related to the toileting routine, a video model of the proper toileting sequence may be helpful. As most children tend to forget some aspect of the toileting routine at some time, most children can benefit from video modeling. In order to help William to remember all of the steps, we decided to make a video model. As you can imagine, no one offered to help act this out, so I had to do it myself. I talked my way through the steps and modeled as much as I could. It went something like this: "When I go to the bathroom, first I close the door (modeled), then I lift the lid (modeled), then I lift the seat (modeled), then I pull down my pants (not modeled), then I pee (modeled by squirting water from a water bottle into the toilet – I made sure the water bottle couldn't be seen), then I pull up by pants (not modeled), then I put down the seat (modeled), then I put down the lid (modeled), then I flush (modeled), then I wash and dry my hands (not modeled)." The video model worked almost instantly. For a girl, after "I pull down my pants," I might say, "Then, I sit down." Be sure to capture the perspective of turning from facing the toilet to turning in the other direction. After that, continue facing away from the toilet and capture the sound of water being squirted into the toilet, etc.

TURN-TAKING. Board games are great turn-taking activities. I highly recommend videotaping the same board game at least three times because typically the roll of the dice determines the move and this, of course, will not always be the same. Keep the board game out of reach, so that your child cannot practice the same moves he saw on the video. It may be a struggle in the beginning to get him to follow the roll of the dice as opposed to moving the same number of spaces he saw on the video. If you persist, you will probably prevail. As you roll the dice, talk about what number you got and count the move out loud, both when you video and when you play your practice games together. Also, note whose turn it is by calling out "My turn/your turn" while you video. It is probably not necessary to videotape the entire game; that would be fairly boring to watch!

WRITING. If your child is struggling with writing or is having difficulty holding a pencil, video modeling is a great way to let him see how to do it right without a lot of distraction. Note how your child is picking up his pencil. Then, I suggest the following three steps, always zooming in on the pencil grip:

1. Say, "Pick up your pencil," and pick it up as your child would.
2. Then say, "Hold it right (or 'pinch the pencil' or whichever expression is most comfortable to you and your child)," and model how to hold it. Also include a model of picking up the pencil and *quickly* adjusting the grip in response to the command "Pick up your pencil."
3. Then say, "Write your name," and write *his* name (not your name).

At first, I would not expect your child to be able to fully imitate how to write his name, but he may very well memorize this also. If you hold the camcorder in one hand and write with the other, your child may have a better perspective on hand/eye coordination than if you videotape someone else writing his name. We repeated the pencil grip video a number of times in different ways until he finally understood it.

Generally, I never model behaviors I don't want imitated. Picking up a pencil as your child does is acceptable because typically after we pick up a pencil, we have to adjust the grip.

If your child is having difficulty with writing too hard or too light, he may be able to understand your verbal instructions if you model the difference between writing harder and writing lighter on video.

YES/NO QUESTIONS. There are many aspects to this lesson.

You can model a nod for yes and a headshake for no. Simply, push RECORD and tell your actor to *show me yes/no* and videotape the nod or headshake. The video will probably be more powerful if you give your actor a reward such as positive praise or an edible reinforcer *after he shows the yes and no.* When you practice the yes/no lesson, it will also be helpful to give your child the same positive praise or edible reinforcer.

You can also teach your child to answer yes or no to whether or not he wants something. We started with objects that we knew William would say yes to, such as "Q: Do you want a candy? A: Yes (with a simultaneous nod of the head)." It may be more motivating to watch this if the person who is answering *yes* to the question receives the object he says *yes* to.

If your child says *yes* to the object that you selected for an obvious *no* response, give the child the item. It is important to respond accordingly to the *yes* and *no* answers of your child. For example, if you are confident that your child will respond "no" when asked if he wants a binder clip (who would want a binder clip) and instead he says "yes," give him the binder clip.

And finally, there is the true/false aspect of the lesson. The standard question and answer format is as follows: "Q: Is this a (object) A: (Yes or No, depending on which way you asked the question)."

CONCLUSION

As with implementing any methodology or technique, there is a learning curve. The parent or teacher needs to learn the "how to" of teaching successfully with video modeling. Once the parent or teacher is skilled, the student will need time to adjust to a new way of learning. This could take a day or a few weeks. This could take one video modeling attempt or several. Video modeling, like any other methodology, will work very well for some parents, teachers and children and not so well for others. As it is a teaching method that is visual, predictable and provides control to the child, there is a good probability that it will be a successful strategy for many children with autism.

While this technique first started at home with my son, the majority of preschoolers with autism that I taught also benefited from video modeling. A few of the preschoolers in our program didn't like videos in general. However, even they showed some surprise and amazement at how their teacher and toys could be in the television, while also sitting beside them. This indicates that there may be activities that could be introduced via video more effectively than in person. For these children, there may be more involved in initially encouraging and developing the interest in learning from videos.

In general, encouraging a sense of wonder and interest is fundamental to learning and also to helping to develop a desire to learn. Once the teacher or parent finds the spark, whether it is a teaching method in general or a particular approach to video modeling, it is up to the teacher or parent to brainstorm to keep the learning momentum going.

All children are different. In using video modeling to teach preschoolers with autism in the public school system, the videos that we developed varied from child to child. Most children showed an interest to the videos at the first *screening*. Thereafter, if their interest waned, we made a new video. Somehow, it is much easier to recognize a "dud" effort at teaching when it is visible in the form of a video.

In using video modeling with the preschoolers, it became clear that video modeling is a great way to review lessons before they are presented to children. Video modeling also provides teachers a form of supervision in how paraprofessionals present lessons. The goal is for the paraprofessional to practice the lesson with the child in the manner that it is presented in the video. If the paraprofessional sees the lesson modeled (by the teacher in the video) as often as the child does, which is typically more times than if the lesson were being taught one-to-one, then there is a greater likelihood that the paraprofessional will practice in the manner intended.

Try video modeling or find a friend, teacher or relative that will help you. At some point you will need help with video modeling whether with filming or acting. In general, people like to help and also like to know that they were helpful. You may find that, at first, the people that you ask to help are uncertain about their abilities. If they are able to see success in the form of progress in your child, they will gain confidence and the process will snowball. People delight in knowing that they made a difference.

With all the stresses in our modern world, hopefully, this approach to teaching children with autism will make teaching and learning a less frustrating, more enjoyable process for both you and your child.